JACK SHIT

NUMBER

The Ultimate in Toilet Humour

TREVOR DE SILVA & STEVE ALLEN

summersdale

JACK SHIT: NUMBER 2

Summersdale Publishers Ltd
46 West Street
Chichester
West Sussex
PO19 1RP
UK
www.summersdale.com

Printed and bound in China

ISBN: 978-1-84953-774-2

Substantial discounts on bulk quantities of Summersdale books are available to corporations, professional associations and other organisations. For details contact Nicky Douglas by telephone: +44 (0) 1243 756902, fax: +44 (0) 1243 786300 or email: nicky@summersdale.com.

Introduction

Jack's back!

He's here to salute what is, perhaps, the most useful word in the English language.

From everyday expletive to adjective, and from verb to noun – this is true linguistic dexterity.

Add to this an unparalleled application in simile and metaphor, and the scope of those four little letters becomes apparent.

The following pages recognise and celebrate this scatological achievement.

Enjoy!

Ape shit

Horse shit

Rat shit

Bullshitter

Shit canned

Shit's going down

You're shit 'n'
you know you are...

... you're shit 'n'
you know you are

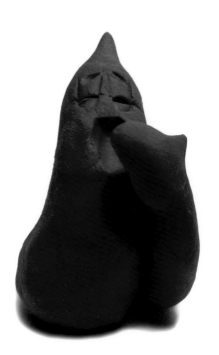

Bored shitless

Look like shit

Shit for brains

Shoot the shit

Welcome

TO

SHITSVILLE

Twinned with
VILLAGES *de* MERDE

Shitsville

Shit hole

Too old for this shit

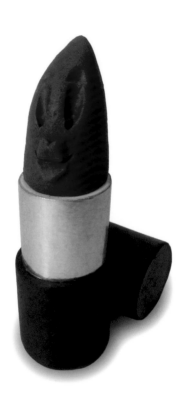

Shit stick

Talking shit

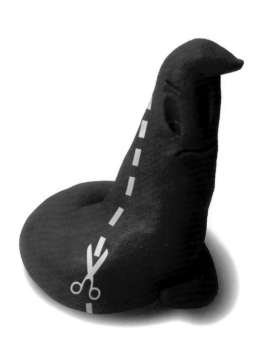

Cut the shit

Lucky shit

Shit out of luck

Bunch of shits

Shiitake

Pig in shit

Built like a
brick shit house

Shit happens

Shitting bricks

Tough shit

Gob shite

Thick as shit

Shit load

Same shit...

... different day

Shit or bust

Dip shit

Seriously deep shit

Bag of shite

Shit shoveller

Shit or get off the pot

Mountain of shit

Shit end of the stick

Shit-kicker

Shit house

Do bears
shit in the woods?

Shit fight

Take a shit

Tear shit up

The Shits

Now wash your hands

If you're interested in finding out more about our books, find us on Facebook at **Summersdale Publishers** and follow us on Twitter at **@Summersdale**.

www.summersdale.com